Generosity IS THE HEART OF God

DR. RUTH W. SMITH

Generosity IS THE HEART OF God

DR. RUTH W. SMITH

Lithonia, GA

© Copyright 2022 – Ruth W. Smith

All rights reserved. No part of this publication may be reproduced, stored in a retrieval system or transmitted in any form or by any means, electronic, mechanical, photocopying, recording or otherwise, without the expressed written permission of the author or publisher.
Scripture references are taken from the King James Version of the Holy Bible unless otherwise noted.

Pronouns for referring to the Father, Son and Holy Spirit are capitalized intentionally, and the words devil and satan are never capitalized.

Publisher: MEWE, LLC
Lithonia, GA
www.mewellc.com

Generosity Is the Heart of God
First Edition
ISBN: 978-1-7360565-6-1

For Worldwide Distribution
Printed in the USA

To God the Father, God the Son, God the Holy Spirit, my beautiful children, including all my seed, the Body of Christ, Light of the World Christian Tabernacle International, Light of the World Covenant Fellowship International, and all of humanity that God so loved that He gave His Son to die for and His Spirit as a constant companion.

May we purpose to live our lives WALKING IN A SPIRIT OF GENEROSITY.

TABLE OF CONTENT

Introduction ix

A Voice that Opens Doors... 1

Foundational Principles of Giving................................. 2

    Sowing... 3

    Reaping a Harvest.. 7

    Tithing 9

    First Fruits 12

    Prophetic Giving.. 13

Priming Your Pump... 15

About the Author... 17

Contact Information.. 19

INTRODUCTION

In order to understand the power of giving in God's economy, I want you to know this key kingdom principle: generosity is the heart of God. For this, we're going to stand on John 3:16:

For God so loved the world that he gave His only begotten Son that whosoever believe in Him shall not perish but have everlasting life (NKJV).

I'm going to paraphrase it a little different: *"For God so loved the world that He was generous and gave His best for us."* His love for us started with His giving. His generosity goes way beyond what we can see because He has protected us from dangers we didn't even know were happening. He was generous with His mercy. He was also generous with His faithfulness toward us.

As you read this booklet, I pray that this spirit of generosity is imparted to you.

- Dr. Ruth W. Smith

When we think about giving or being generous in our sowing, there are so many scriptures that deal with generosity, but first and foremost, the thing I want us to be generous with is our love for one another.

Our love for one another is so critical because what does it profit us to gain everything we can put our hands on, and then lose our souls? Matthew 16:26 reads, *"And what do you benefit if you gain the whole world but lose your own soul?"* When we are not generous towards one another in our love, we are in danger of losing our souls. The Bible states, *"Your love for one another will prove to the world that you are my disciples"* (John 13:35).

A Voice that Opens Doors

You could say that generosity even has a voice. It opens doors for you. It speaks for you – it has a voice. I can think of the many times someone was trying to meet with me, and it wasn't a good time. I would say, "Oh, no. I can't see them right now."

Then the staff would go back to them and tell me, "They just have something they want to give you." Now how could I turn them away? So I would say, "Okay, tell them to just come on in for just a minute."

Well, guess what else happened? Once they got in there with their gift, they were able to say, "Dr. Ruth …" and proceed to tell me what was on their mind. And do you know what I did? I listened because their gift had made a way and spoken for them.

Proverbs 18:16 states, *"A man's gift maketh room for him, and bringeth him before great men."*

You see, your generosity will speak on your behalf. It will open the door for you when typically, you might not have had the chance to walk into in at that moment. But because you were generous, the door opened, and you were able to get to the person.

So, your generosity has a voice and speaks. In fact, your generosity speaks volumes. Whatever you are doing with your generous ways, you have to remember it's sending a message.

The question is: what kind of message is my generosity sending?

Foundational Principles of Giving

Now, the ways in which we express our generosity in God's economy are some of the foundational things I want to share with you in this section.

1. Sowing

The first foundation is seed sowing. I'm a farm girl, so I know a lot about sowing seeds. When you sow seeds, you expect something to come up. Whenever we're planting in the garden, in the field, or whatever ground we sow, we watch over it because we know that something ought to be happening.

People of God, we have to grow to the place where we no longer just scatter our seeds on any ground. We have to be intentional in *where* we sow. We also have to remember to water and watch over our seeds and look out for that harvest with expectation. As you read this, I want you to lift up your expectations. One of the things that God spoke to me was, "Share with the people to hit the reset button on their generosity. This is going to open the door for them to have increase."

What is the reset button? It's discarding our old thinking and adopting a whole new mindset towards our giving.

So, God is saying, "Hit your reset button in this season." Don't just be casual about it. Many of us have sown much, some of us with our very lives. Many of us have sown with our health because we were unfaithful in our care and maintenance. Many of us have sown with our family relations because we were trying to do the will of God but in the wrong place, neglecting our commitments to loved ones.

I'm saying to us that we have to make sure that we hit the reset button today because God wants to do so much more through your life. And to do more, you need more.

There are things that God is trying to do in our lives even now. He wants to open doors for us to have access to more. God may even want to shift our present job so that it doesn't interfere with His assignment. That doesn't mean walking away from your job before God tells you; but it does mean that we have to stay open to allow God to do more with our lives.

I will never forget when the Lord spoke to me about leaving corporate America. I was making a great deal of money, and loved what I was doing, without having to work too hard. It was a great assignment, and I was enjoying just the best of times. And then the Lord said, "I need you to leave to go and undergird the ministry." In fact, He said, "If you don't go and run the ministry from the back offices, it's not going to exist." And then He added, "The structure of the ministry is critical and if it is not structured on a foundation that will survive the test of time, with all the issues, conflicts and dynamics affecting it, it will crash … I have raised you in pharaoh's house and I want you to take the gifts and graces that I've taught you and proven through your hands to where I'm placing you. I want you to take it to my kingdom and establish the Light of the World on that foundation because everything that works is nothing but my Word. I want you to take my treasures back to my house."

But I protested, "God, I can't do that. I have five kids and none of them are in college yet. And then there's my spouse and the medical coverage – there are just so many things ..." I sent a laundry list to the Holy Ghost. The Lord assured me that He was not playing any games and that I could leave in obedience, because He was able to set it up on my behalf.

So, I said, "All right! I'll do it," and then I added, "But look, if You want me to do it, if this is of You, I need insurance and I need the company to cover me. And I need to be able to return to this job if the plan does not work. And I need …" I continued to give some other specifics. That was a Friday. Come Monday morning, there was a document on my desk from the Benefits Office that read: Sabbatical - New Offer. It had never been offered before because corporations had not even started making such offers.

In the midst of my petitioning God and putting out that fleece before Him, the door opened for more discussion. "You have to be vested already," HR said. Well, I was already vested. "You have to be surplussed," they went on. I wasn't surplussed – but I knew I could negotiate that bit. And finally, they said, "You can return back to work after a year or after two years or three years, and your insurance will stay in place."

God allowed all of the things that I so desperately needed. He checked all the boxes. And so I went to my manager, and said, "I'm leaving." The rest of the story is history. I left.

Why am I telling all this? Because you just have to know that when God is speaking to you, He will move you into the best of situations. Because, people of God, hear this: you've earned every penny, every benefit, every privilege that is extended to you – you'd better believe you paid for it over time. Sometimes you paid for it double time.

I could never have imagined that plan of God for my life. From that moment, I've been around the world and doing ministry everywhere. Somebody was talking to me the other day about not working so hard, and I said, "I don't work. I haven't worked for 30 years. I'm enjoying every minute of what I'm doing, and it doesn't feel like work to me."

My friend, God has a plan for your life. What He wants to establish in you is to learn to be generous. Don't hoard. Just be generous. Just be open and let God be God. Test Him and try Him. Don't be afraid. You can recognize His voice and listen. Don't listen to people telling you not to put a fleece before God. If your faith should bend, you need a fleece put and pinned out there. God is big enough to handle your fleece – if that's what you need. Sometimes, our faith is all stirred up and we're ready to go and take that step. Other times, we take a step back and wait to make sure of what God is saying.

2. Reaping a Harvest

I want you to read Mark 4:26-29:

He also said, "A man scatters seed on the ground. Night and day, whether he sleeps or gets up, the seed sprouts and grows, though he does not know how. All by itself the soil produces grain—first the stalk, then the head, then the full kernel in the head. As soon as the grain is ripe, he puts the sickle to it, because the harvest has come."

This scripture is not about the process of planting. It's about the harvest. If we plant a field, we should expect a harvest in due season; in fact, if we plant anything, you should expect a harvest. Therefore, if we are sowing good seed, we should expect good to return on our investment.

Now, by the same token, if we sow wickedness, we are going to harvest wickedness. So be on guard when something is not your harvest because the enemy will try and send you a harvest that doesn't belong to you. The enemy is trying to force it on you. You have to learn how to be able to stand flat-footed and straight forward, looking people or things in the eye and say, "That is not my harvest" – because you know how you have sown.

So be assured that if you sow, there is a harvest that's going to come back from your sowing. Let's make sure that we expect the harvest because the enemy likes to tell us that nothing is coming of what we are doing, and he tries to make us quit before time.

Take fasting, for instance, the devil will stop you from fasting just before the fast is over to prevent your breakthrough. The Lord had called me on a fast a few weeks ago. I obeyed, but I decided to pause the fast on the weekend. So, Saturday came and we were ready to go out for lunch. Then the Lord said, "Who told you not to fast on the weekend?" Out of obedience, I went back and continued fasting. Well, I tell you, that night something in the atmosphere broke. Only God could have done it. That Saturday night, there were all kind of messages to my phone telling me of breakthroughs, taking down demonic fortresses, and testimonies of deliverance.

God said to me, "This is why you couldn't quit. If you had quit prematurely, the breakthrough on Saturday night wouldn't have happened. The only reason it happened is because you persisted and took the head off of the enemy." Halleluiah! We've got to be ready to fight the good fight of faith!

Any time you sow a seed, you should expect the harvest to come up. Don't give up.

3. Tithing

The third principle is tithing. Tithing is another expression of generosity. And you can always tell the people that tithe. The other day somebody was trying to "educate" me that we do not have to tithe in this dispensation. I can always tell when a person is not fully informed because they start their sentences typically with something that's not accurate. They often start off with, "Tithing only started with the law of Moses." Well, I knew right away how misinformed they were because tithing didn't start with the law. It started long before the law. The first example of tithing we have is when Abraham gave Melchizedek a tenth of all the spoil after battle (see Genesis 14:20). When Abraham gave to Melchizedek – who was a shadow of Christ – it was the lesser giving to the greater. This activated the principle of blessing. It had nothing to do with the law.

All the same, I thought about tithing some more, and I went back to the Word and meditated on what I read. In that time, the Lord said, "Don't let nobody tell you how to not get blessed." You see, this principle is a principle of blessing. Whether it's the law or not, it's still a principle of blessing.

According to Malachi 3:9, when we don't give God that portion that belongs to Him, we put ourselves under a curse. Even if we have been blessed, so to speak, and are receiving income, we can still put a limit on what God wants to do for us. I believe the only reason that I have personally thrived financially in these hard times is because of the principle of giving God what's due to Him first of all.

Understand that tithing is important, but it's just the beginning. The flow of being generous has just been released. But, of course, if I just gave 10% and feel I have arrived, then I would be doing it as unto the law – as an act of legalism. But I don't do it that way. I give back as a foundational principle. Even if I haven't been at church, my tithes are set up on autopay. It doesn't matter whether I come to the church building or not, my tithes still go to the church automatically.

On the other hand, what if I said that I don't have to be a tither and don't have to be systematic in my giving? That means if I do not come to church this week, I give nothing. No, that should not be the case. That's why God set a standard that we should step up to and be faithful in our giving even when things go awry. This is why systematic giving is so critical. I don't have to come to the church to give my offering. I have it set up to give automatically.

And do you know what? When I see that deduction in my account, I say, "Glory to God!" Since it is automatic, it comes straight out of my account, and I start celebrating before God. I say, "God, You're faithful and I'm grateful!"

This is no time for me to be letting up on my giving especially with the trouble that arises all over the world. I'm telling you, all this giving works together for our good. Faithfulness works. Generosity works.

There's something about the first – it's off the top, before you do anything else. We have our bills on auto pay, and we ought to have giving on auto pay too, so nothing gets in front of our giving to God.

Halleluiah!

4. First Fruits

Now in addition to our regular *tithes* and *offering,* we also give our first fruits. In the Old Testament, first fruits referred to offering the initial part of the harvest to the Lord to receive His blessing for the full harvest. For us new covenant believers, first fruits is a substantial amount we give when we receive a blessing. whether in the form of a bonus, a salary raise, a gift, or even the start of a new season (see Numbers 18:13).

Different churches have their way of interpreting the amount and the place to give, but the principle behind first fruits is always the same: we acknowledge that God is the owner of everything we possess.

Generosity is at the heart of first fruits. Proverbs 3:9-10 talks about honoring the Lord with the first fruits of our blessing:

> *Honor the LORD with your wealth, with the firstfruits of all your crops; then your barns will be filled to overflowing, and your vats will brim over with new wine.*

Every new year, I always like to present my first fruits before the Lord because the Bible says that if you give of the first, the whole loaf is holy. All the rest of the year will be sanctified. I've seen God multiply money for me so that I know this is nothing but the hand of God.

You need to hit the reset button, so God can bring increase to your life in His amazing way. It's just as important that we give with understanding. We can't give out of ignorance because it denies the full flow of the blessing. It's true, people do give because we charge them to, but they, themselves, need to dig in to fully understand the truth of God's promise about the increase.

5. Prophetic Giving

One of the most powerful types of generosity is prophetic giving. Prophetic giving is giving to the man and woman of God to meet their personal needs. And I'm going to testify a little bit on this point because I have this grace of prophetic giving. Sometimes I can see the needs of the man or woman of God and my heart goes out to assist them. They don't have to ask me – I just sense the need.

One day, I saw the former pastor of my church with his legs crossed. When I looked at the underside of his shoes, they had holes in them. "Wait," I said to myself, "that's our pastor and his shoes have holes in the bottom." After church, we would always go and chat with him. "Pastor," what size of shoes do you wear?" I asked one day. He told me. Later, I went to a store in the mall and inquired about the best type of men's shoes. The salesman told me Stacy Adams were the best, so I got him three pairs – brown, black, and gray. I brought these shoes back to the church and gave them to him. No strings attached. It was nothing personal. It was simply that he was a man of God who represented us before God and before God's people.

Church – our pastor represents us! And it's important that we care for them as well. But it's a grace – not everyone is supposed to do that. God is faithful in how He would help you to show generosity towards the man and woman of God. Did you know about that giving? Don't be timid about being generous to the man and woman of God.

Just make sure God says it and that you're not expecting anything in return.

As for me, I want the man or woman of God to have a mind free from encumbrances. I want them to have clear access to the Holy Ghost without all kinds of anxieties and concerns. So, when they preach, they are not preaching from their issues, their lacks, and their brokenness. They are speaking life into our lives so we can get all the breakthroughs we need. I admit it may seem a little self-centered, but I want them to have clarity of vision for my benefit.

Therefore, when you have a prompting to do something for the man and woman of God, go and do it. They should be the person that's preparing, equipping, and causing you to soar. Generosity is at the heart of God. Let that be your heart too.

Prime Your Pump

Now, here's what God wanted me to do. He wanted me to help you hit the reset button for your life. Here's how. As you know, I grew up in rural Alabama where we didn't have running water. So, we had a pump. You had to pour water into the pump in order to get it going; it was called "priming the pump." My daddy used to tell us, "Whenever you finish, do not use the last water." That was a little water cup sitting by the pump that we used to just fill it up and set it back. It didn't take much. He said, "Make sure you fill the cup back up because otherwise, we can't get the pump to get started again."

Well, that principle stuck with me. And that's why I want you to set aside a small sum of money for your giving – look at it as the little cup of water that primes the pump. I want you to never spend it. It's not for spending; it's for storing. It's not that we're worshiping money, for money is simply a method of exchange in this realm, and there's nothing wrong with exchange.

I want you to put it away in a safe place so that you will always have the water to prime the pump. So when the devil tells you that you don't have anything, when the devil tells you you're broke, when the devil tells you you're busted, when the devil tells you that you aren't going to thrive, when the devil tells you there's not going to be enough, you are able to say, "Look demon, you are a liar because I am not broke. I have my priming money and I understand the power of giving in God's economy and I will never give out, in Jesus' name." Halleluiah! Glory to God!

ABOUT THE AUTHOR

Dr. Ruth W. Smith, a native of Greensboro, Alabama, accepted Christ in 1964 and was filled with the Holy Spirit in 1981. She married Pastor Jimmie Lee Smith in 1982. Answering the call to the ministry in 1990, she co-founded Light of the World Christian Tabernacle International and Light of the World Covenant Fellowship International and was later ordained as a minister in 1991.

Under the dynamic leadership of Pastors Jimmie Lee and Ruth W. Smith, The Light grew from 400 to 1,500 members in a 4-year period until Archbishop Jimmie Lee Smith went home to be with the Lord in 2008. The stirring mission of the ministry is to "See a World Without Darkness."

Light of the World Covenant Fellowship International is an organization that mentors and empowers Pastors and Ministries throughout the world. Dr. Ruth was consecrated Archbishop of the organization on July 13, 2008 and became the first woman to serve a worldwide Diocese, overseeing ministries in 26 countries with a membership of over 200,000.

Dr. Ruth's passion for helping people advance the Kingdom of God started from an early age when she participated in the integration of schools in Hale County, Alabama. Through her leadership at The Light, she champions community support through food and clothing drives. In 2013, she received the "Torch Bearer" award by the Southern Christian Leadership Conference (SCLC) in Washington, DC, in recognition of her many years of work as a scholar and spiritual leader committed to the legacy of SCLC founder, Dr. Martin Luther King, Jr.

She recently opened the Jimmie Lee Smith Community Center (JLSCC), which provides Sports, Education and Entertainment to the surrounding communities. Additionally, she established three SateLight locations: LOTW Decatur, December 2015; LOTW South, April 2016; and LOTW Gwinnett, December 2016.

Dr. Ruth holds a Master's degree in Biblical Counseling and a Doctorate in Ministry from Biblical Life College and Seminary in Marshfield, Missouri. She is the published author of four other books, *A Word on Love*, *Keep Moving*, *Rules of Encouragement*, and *The Voice*.

She is the proud mother of five children, twelve grandchildren and four great-grandchildren, whom she dearly loves. She is anointed to preach and teach the gospel of Jesus Christ, which she does readily worldwide. Her foundational scripture is Romans 8:28, *"For we know that all things work together for good to them that love God, to them who are the called according to His purpose."*

CONTACT INFORMATION

Ministry
Light of the World Christian Ministries
5883 Highway 155 North
Stockbridge, GA 30281
678.565.7001
thelight@comeintothelight.org
www.comeintothelight.org

Purchasing
678.565.7001
www.comeintothelight.org

Publisher
MEWE, LLC
404.482.3135
mewecorporation@gmail.com
www.mewellc.com

www.ingramcontent.com/pod-product-compliance
Lightning Source LLC
Chambersburg PA
CBHW030047100526
44590CB00011B/350